Manage Your Time

SUPER QUICK SKILLS

Manage Your Time

Kaye Rabel

Los Angeles | London | New Delhi
Singapore | Washington DC | Melbourne

Los Angeles | London | New Delhi
Singapore | Washington DC | Melbourne

SAGE Publications Ltd
1 Oliver's Yard
55 City Road
London EC1Y 1SP

SAGE Publications Inc.
2455 Teller Road
Thousand Oaks, California 91320

SAGE Publications India Pvt Ltd
B 1/I 1 Mohan Cooperative Industrial Area
Mathura Road
New Delhi 110 044

SAGE Publications Asia-Pacific Pte Ltd
3 Church Street
#10-04 Samsung Hub
Singapore 049483

First published 2021

Editor: Jai Seaman
Assistant editor: Lauren Jacobs
Production editor: Rachel Burrows
Marketing manager: Catherine Slinn
Cover design: Shaun Mercier
Typeset by: C&M Digitals (P) Ltd, Chennai, India
Printed in the UK

Library of Congress Control Number: 2020942656

British Library Cataloguing in Publication data

A catalogue record for this book is available from the British Library

ISBN 978-1-5297-4258-9

Contents

Everything in this book!

Section 1 What is time management?

Many students experience challenges with finding time to get everything done. This section provides an overview of time management and how learning these strategies will help you during your studies and beyond.

Section 2 Why is time management important for writing projects?

You will complete many writing projects during your studies. In this section, you will learn that managing your time to write is imperative for completing writing assignments on time and with quality.

Section 3 How do I manage my time for writing projects?

Avoiding procrastination and managing your time in writing projects is an important component of success in your studies. This section provides an overview of the PSTI time management process.

Section 4 How do I determine what I need to do?

The type of writing project that you are working on will determine exactly what you need to do. This section shows you how to decide what you need to do based on the type of writing assignment.

Section 5 How do I plan tasks?

Some students find it difficult to get everything done because they aren't sure where to start. This section helps by guiding you through how to plan tasks.

Section 6 How do I set task completion deadlines?

It is important not only to determine what needs to be done, but also to identify when things should be completed. In this section, you will be guided through setting task completion deadlines.

Section 7 How do I stay on track and make sure everything gets done?

Calendars are an effective way to schedule and plan tasks. In this section you will be guided through using a calendar to track task completion.

Section 8 How do I take action to complete tasks?

The purpose of time management is to help you get everything done. Taking action to complete tasks is essential for following the PSTI process. In this section you will pick up tips on completing tasks.

Section 9 How do I manage my time when working with a partner or in a group?

Often jobs require people to work in groups; therefore universities include group work to help students learn to work with others. In this section, you will learn more about managing your time when working in groups.

Section 10 How do I manage my time while balancing academic and other life priorities?

Students also have other priorities in life besides writing projects. This section expands on applying time management to other areas of your life including work, attending to family matters as well as your social life.

Section 11 DIY: Putting it all together

This section includes activities, reflections and hands-on exercises that guide you through implementing the PSTI process in your current writing projects. Very soon you will be on your way to managing your writing projects and all areas of your life more effectively.

SECTION ONE

What is time management?

10 second summary

Time management means employing strategies and tools to ensure you use your time wisely, in turn making sure you get done everything you want to.

60 second summary

Time is a precious resource

You can't get it back once it is gone so it is important to use your time wisely.

Management means using strategies to ensure something operates properly and runs smoothly. If you work or have an internship, your manager or supervisor 'manages' your work to make sure you perform assigned tasks correctly.

Time management works in a similar way. It means using strategies to ensure you do all the things that need to get done. Time management equips you with tools and a schedule to follow to complete tasks.

This book will help you learn strategies to manage your time at university and beyond.

What are the tasks in my life?

We live in a time when there are so many things going on that compete for our attention. These things include not only our coursework at university, but spending time with family, friends or a significant other and maybe also a job or internship.

We need to balance these with our own needs, including time to relax, watch some TV or scroll through our social media feeds.

The first step in managing your time is to undertstand all the tasks in your life. The day-to-day tasks that you complete can be categorized as *essential*, *compelling* or *leisure*.

Types of tasks

- **Essential** – things that you must get done (e.g. eating, paying bills, attending lectures)
- **Compelling** – things that are important to you and enrich your life (e.g. cultural or faith-based activities, voluntary work, helping a friend)
- **Leisure** – things you do for fun or to relax (e.g. going to the cinema, going out to eat, listening to music).

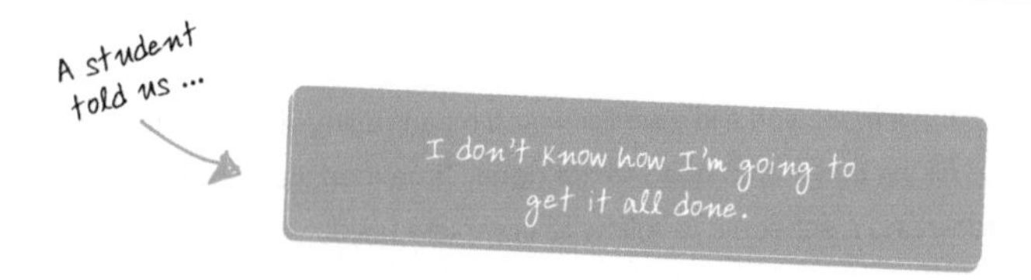

Why is managing my time important?

Our lives are full of distractions. Today, smartphones have so many different apps including games and social media, as well as incoming calls and text messages that it can be difficult to stay focused and keep on track to do everything that you need to.

Time management gives you the skills to complete necessary tasks as well as making time for fun.

Risks of not managing your time include:

- Forgetting to complete an assignment
- Being late for work or an appointment
- Feeling disappointed for overlooking something or letting someone down.

The benefits include:

- Increased quality of course assignments
- Being punctual
- Reducing stress.

Managing your time helps to ensure you give yourself enough time to complete course assignments properly. Devoting time to meeting all the requirements of an assignment can increase the quality of your work.

Time management can help with arriving on time for lectures, work and other appointments.

Waiting until the last minute to complete assignments or not having a plan for completing tasks causes stress. When you are stressed, your body produces a hormone called cortisol. The presence of this hormone in the body inhibits your ability to think clearly. This adversely affects your mental health and may cause you to worry or have anxiety. Using these strategies helps to reduce stress because you won't have to worry about how you will get everything done.

What's an example of time management?

Megan studies Education and works part-time as a waitress. To help keep everything sorted, each week Megan looks ahead and does the following:

- Checks her course outline to see what assignments are due
- Checks her work rota
- Sees what social commitments she has made with friends
- Makes a list of all the tasks she needs to do for the week.

Megan's look ahead

Megan reviews her course outline and notices she has an essay on pedagogical strategies due in 3 weeks. Megan wants to start planning her essay so she has enough time to do a good job. In her Early Childhood course, Megan notices 2 discussion posts due by the end of the week. Megan then makes a list for the week including the 3 evenings she is scheduled to work:

Megan's list

- Lectures and tutorials on Monday, Tuesday and Thursday
- Plan and start researching pedagogical strategies for essay

- Make 2 discussion board posts in Early Childhood Education course
- Work Wednesday, Friday and Saturday evening shifts.

After creating the list Megan's next steps are to:

- Determine how much time each task will take
- Schedule the tasks in her calendar.

In summary, the overall process looks like this:

1. Looking ahead to see what assignments are due
2. Identifying other upcoming essential tasks
3. Identifying compelling and leisure tasks
4. Making a list of all the tasks that need to be completed this week
5. Determining how much time the tasks will take
6. Scheduling the tasks in a calendar.

This example provides a quick snapshot of how you will learn to manage your time.

Don't get in a bind, manage your time!

CHECK POINT Why should I manage my time?

Try these multiple choice questions to test your understanding. Choose *one option* in question 1 and *two options* in question 2:

1 Time management is

a Relying on your memory to determine the day's tasks

b Looking ahead and prioritizing when to complete upcoming tasks

c Completing tasks based on how much time you have in a given day

2 Benefits of managing your time include

a Less stress worrying about forgetting to complete an assignment

b Knowing each week what needs to be completed and when

c Anxiety as a result of seeing everything that needs to be done

Answers:

1 b

2 a and b

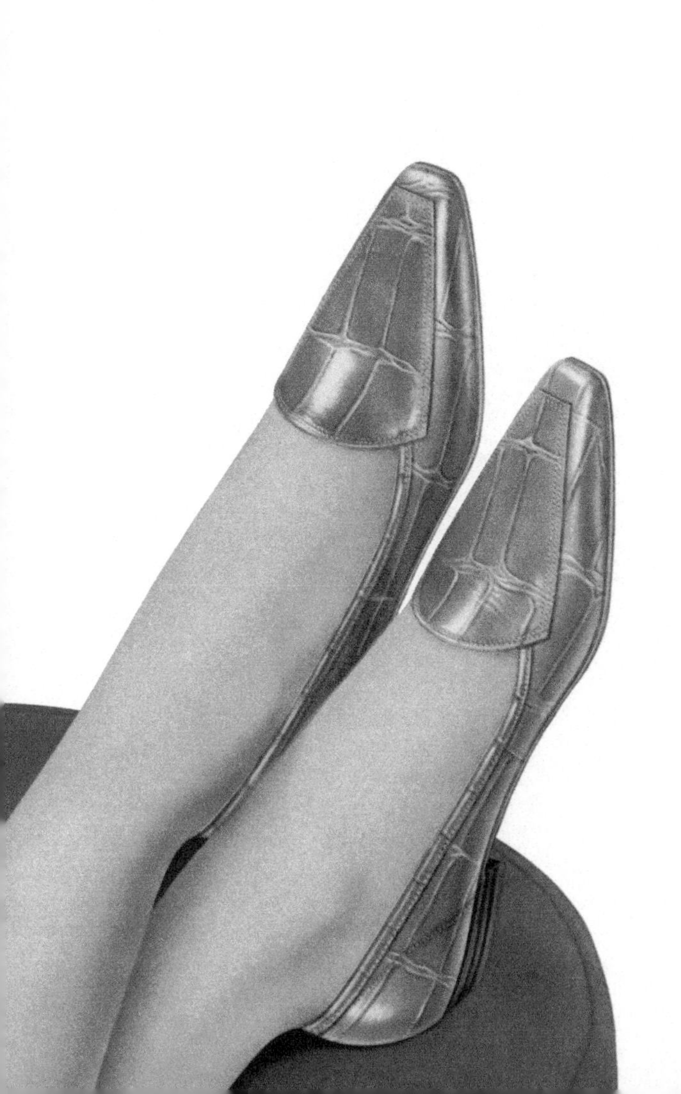

SECTION TWO

Why is time management important for writing projects?

10 second summary

Writing is a major part of your studies and time management helps you do your best work.

60 second summary

Time management is essential

Time management is an important part of being successful in academia. It helps you ensure you are using your time effectively to write essays, papers and other written assignments. It is an essential skill when working on more extensive projects such as theses or dissertations, when the project could take several months or even years to complete.

Writing is a big part of the academic process. Writing projects are tools to help students learn. They also help tutors assess how much students have learnt. Managing your time to write is imperative in successfully completing quality written assignments on time.

How does writing help you learn?

We receive information from our environment via our senses. This information is interpreted and transferred to the area of the brain responsible for *short-term memory* storage. Short-term memory doesn't keep information for a very long time; it only stores it briefly. If information isn't processed further by the brain, it will be forgotten: if you don't use it, you lose it!

However, when the brain does some extra work to process information it moves into what is called *long-term memory*. This is a process responsible for remembering and the information will not be easily forgotten. Learning results from information moving into the long-term memory.

Writing is one mechanism through which the brain moves information from short-term to long-term memory.

Plan for success by making a plan!

How can writing show what you have learnt?

In academia writing is often used as an assessment tool to evaluate learning. The writing you do as part of your coursework tells a story of your level of understanding of a topic. Your writing at various stages throughout your time as a student communicates how much you have learnt. This includes what you've learnt about a topic or concept during a module as well as over an entire course.

- **Concept or topic level** – Writing an essay evaluates topic-level learning, such as how much someone has learnt during a week of a course.
- **Course level** – A written term or semester exam evaluates module-level learning, such as how much someone has learnt during the module.
- **Programme level** – Writing a thesis or dissertation evaluates course-level learning, such as how much someone has learnt while completing a bachelor's or master's degree.

The table below provides an example of how different writing assignments or projects can show how much you have learnt.

Concept or topic level	Module level	Course level
• Discussion board post • Essay • Weekly writing assignments • Literature review	• Research paper • Case study • Written term or semester exams	• Capstone project • Thesis or dissertation

As we can see above, writing is a major part of academic study. It is important to do your best on your writing projects because writing helps you learn and shows what you've learnt.

Planning as well as working through the writing process takes time. Managing your time to write helps you:

- Plan effectively when you will complete the phases of the writing process
- Prevents procrastination and helps you avoid stress
- Helps you do your best work by giving yourself enough time to write.

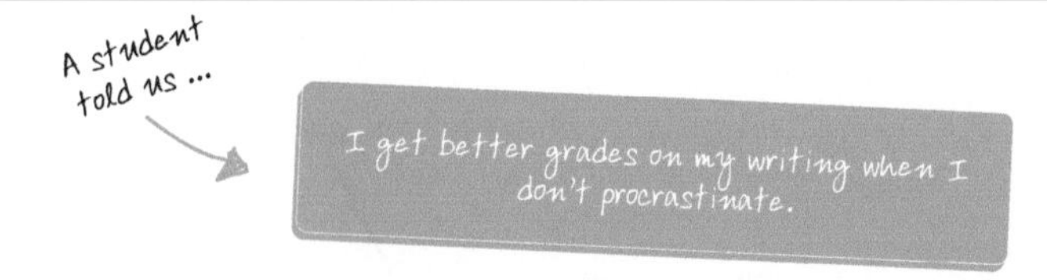

Try these multiple choice questions to test your understanding. For each question, choose the two best responses:

1 Why are writing projects an important part of your studies?

a Writing projects help universities track how much time students spend on coursework

b Writing helps the brain further process information so it can be remembered

c Tutors can read what a student wrote and determine what the student learnt about a topic

2 Why should you manage your time?

a To help you learn and show what you learnt in your coursework

b To take control of writing projects and reduce stress

c To do a good job and complete writing projects on time

Answers:

1 b and c

2 b and c

SECTION THREE

How do I manage my time for writing projects?

10 second summary

Managing your time during writing projects includes planning tasks, setting task completion deadlines, taking action and being committed to following the process.

60 second summary

What is the PSTI process?

Procrastination and a lack of preparation are the main two ways students mismanage their time to write. Using time management strategies can help students make the most of their time during writing projects.

PSTI is a quick and easy time management process to follow for your writing projects. Each letter stands for a step in the overall process:

- **P**lanning tasks
- **S**etting task completion deadlines
- **T**aking action to complete tasks
- **I**ntegrity.

Planning tasks involves detailing what needs to be done and estimating how long it will take to complete a task. Setting task completion deadlines includes scheduling tasks on a calendar. Taking action means completing tasks. Integrity is the glue that holds everything together by you committing to follow the process.

Procrastination doesn't pay off

Students have reported mismanaging their time due to procrastination as well as failing to prepare properly. Procrastination occurs when you put off completing writing assignments and find other, less demanding things to do instead. Lack of preparation includes not planning your time to write, not following a writing schedule or waiting until the last minute to complete assignments. Procrastination and lack of preparation usually occur together.

Using the strategies in the PSTI process will help you to be prepared to write and help you avoid waiting until the last minute to work on your writing assignments.

What are common ways in which students mismanage their time?

 Procrastination	 Lack of preparation
• Waiting until 'tomorrow' • Waiting to feel 'creative' • Waiting to be in the 'mood' to write	• Not planning time to write • Not following a writing schedule • Thinking your first draft needs to be perfect

Students often feel like their first draft needs to be perfect. It's called a rough draft for a reason! What is important is to follow the writing process and write. When you use the PSTI process you have time to revisit your first draft and revise it multiple times to make it just right.

What makes up planning tasks?

Planning tasks involves identifying what needs to be done and detailing those tasks. In this step of **P**STI:

- Look ahead to see what writing assignments are due
- Make a list of all upcoming writing assignments
- Determine how much time writing tasks will take.

What makes up setting task completion deadlines?

Setting task completion deadlines involves determining realistic timelines and scheduling tasks. In this step of P**S**TI:

- Schedule writing tasks on a calendar.

My biggest issue with completing my assignments is finding the time to write.

What makes up taking action?

Taking action is just as it sounds. In this step of PST**I**:

- Follow through by completing tasks
- Track the status of task completion.

What does integrity mean for this process?

Think of **integrity** as the ingredient that is sprinkled throughout the entire time management process. In PST**I**, integrity means being accountable and doing what you said you would do during every step. Integrity ensures the process will work!

In summary, managing your time will help you avoid procrastination and help you to be prepared to make the most of your writing time. Planning tasks helps you detail what needs to be done and estimate how long it will take to complete a task. Setting task completion deadlines and scheduling tasks on a calendar help to remind you when to do tasks. Taking action helps to ensure you complete tasks. The entire process is infused with integrity, which ensures you follow through.

Tips for making the most of your writing time include:

- Follow the PSTI process
- When it is time to write, find a quiet location where there will be limited interruptions and distractions
- Put your phone on silent or, if possible, turn your phone off
- Be patient with yourself and follow a writing process (see page 41)
- Don't worry about getting every word perfect in your first draft … you will revise it later
- Follow the schedule that you have created!

Time waits for no one, so make the most of it!

Why should I manage my time for writing projects?

Test your knowledge by answering the following questions.

1. What are the two common ways in which students mismanage their time?

2. Which component of PSTI involves reviewing your course outline and determining what upcoming writing assignments you have?
   - a Planning tasks
   - b Setting task completion deadlines
   - c Taking action to complete tasks
   - d Integrity

3. Which component of PSTI is woven throughout the entire process to ensure you complete each step?
   - a Planning tasks
   - b Setting task completion deadlines
   - c Taking action to complete tasks
   - d Integrity

Answers:
1 Procrastination and lack of preparation
2 a
3 d

SECTION FOUR

How do I determine what I need to do?

10 second summary

In the PSTI process the first step of planning tasks is to identify everything that needs to be done. The type of writing assignment will determine what you need to do.

60 second summary

The type of assignment guides what you need to do

You will identify the tasks that you need to do based on the type of writing assignment. Some writing assignments will only require a few tasks such as writing a weekly discussion board post for an online or hybrid class.

Longer or more comprehensive writing assignments will require more tasks. Writing an essay or doing a literature review includes other components for which you need to plan time to conduct research, review a variety of sources and take notes before you can start writing. You will need to think about these types of tasks in addition to the time you spend writing.

What is an example of determining what I need to do?

In this example, we will identify some typical tasks involved in writing an essay. These include:

1. Selecting a topic
2. Locating sources (e.g. articles, books, websites)
3. Reviewing sources and taking notes
4. Creating an outline
5. Writing a first draft
6. Reviewing and revising your draft
7. Finalizing and submitting your essay.

Selecting a topic

The first step is to review the requirements of the assignment and select an appropriate topic to write about.

Locating sources

Next, you should to go to the library or visit the library online and search for and locate appropriate sources.

Reviewing sources and taking notes

After selecting sources, you need to make time to read the information and take notes.

Creating an outline

After you have gathered all relevant source information, read it and taken notes, the next step is to create an outline of the major sections and content of your essay.

Writing a first draft

Once the outline is complete, it is time to write your first draft. You will most likely need multiple sessions over a few days to complete your draft.

Reviewing and revising your draft

After completing your first draft, review it, checking for cohesiveness, spelling mistakes and grammar issues. Revise the draft accordingly. This may take multiple sessions.

Finalizing and submitting your essay

Lastly, once you have everything in good shape, finalize and submit your essay.

> *Knowing where to start helps you get started!*

Identifying tasks helps put your mind at ease

All the tasks discussed so far take time to complete so be sure to capture everything that will need to be done. Identifying all the tasks helps you break the writing assignment into smaller chunks. Seeing the smaller pieces makes the writing tasks much more manageable and helps you avoid feeling overwhelmed. Detailing all the tasks will also put your mind at ease because you will have a clear picture of what you need to do.

Once you have identified all the tasks the next step is to estimate how long it will take to complete each one. You will use this information to schedule everything in a calendar and set task completion deadlines which we will review in the next two sections.

A student told us ...

I don't know where to start when I have a writing project.

Additional writing resources

There are many resources that will help with the overall writing process whether you are writing an essay, literature review, or a thesis or dissertation.

The example discussed in this section provides only a general overview. Each task can be further broken down into more sub-tasks. For more information on the specifics of these sub-tasks, you may want to review other titles in the Super Quick Skills series such as *Plan Your Essay*, *Find Your Source*, *Cite Your Source* and *Polish Your Academic Writing*.

Determining what I need to do

Answer the following questions to check your understanding.

1 **True or False** Identifying all of the tasks this way helps you break the writing assignment into smaller chunks.

2 **True or False** All the steps will always be the same, no matter the type of writing project.

Answers:

1 True

2 False

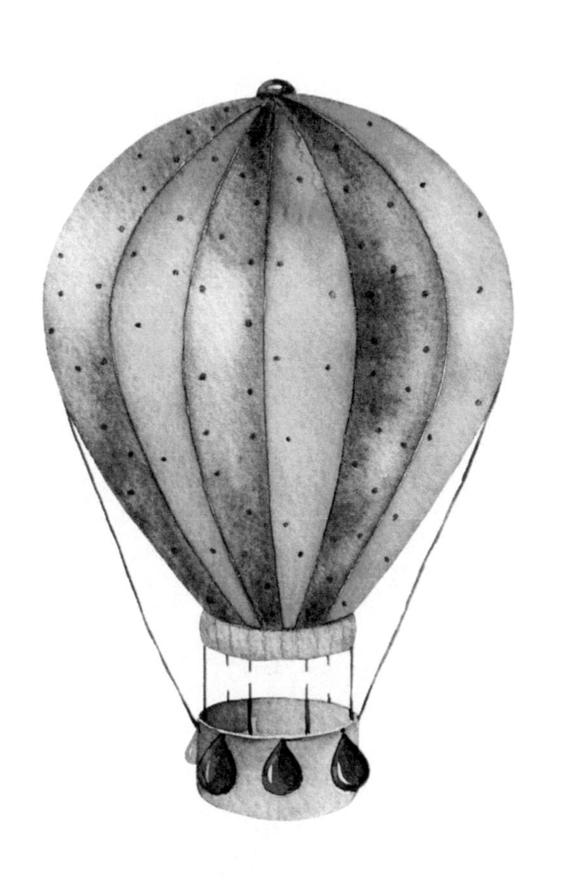

SECTION FIVE

How do I plan tasks?

10 second summary

Now that you've identified some of your writing tasks we will complete the planning process by estimating how long it will take to complete each task.

60 second summary

Planning is the first step

As we previously learnt, planning tasks in the PSTI process involves identifying what needs to be done and detailing those tasks. To complete the planning process you will also estimate how long each task will take to complete. Understanding how long it will take to complete a given task will help you with the next phase of PSTI, which is setting task completion deadlines. You will learn more about this phase in the next section.

What does the planning phase comprise?

During the planning tasks phase of **P**STI you will need to:

- Look ahead to see what writing assignments are due
- Make a list of all upcoming writing assignments
- Detail the tasks you will need to do for each writing assignment
- Estimate how much time it will take to do each task.

It all comes together when you have a plan!

What is an example of planning tasks?

Remember the essay example from Section 5? We'll use those tasks to explore estimating the time it will take to complete each task.

A summary of the typical tasks and time estimates for writing an essay includes the following:

Essay writing tasks	Time estimate
☐ Selecting a topic	1 day
☐ Locating sources (e.g. articles, books, websites)	2 days
☐ Reviewing sources and taking notes	4 sessions over a week
☐ Creating an outline	2 days
☐ Writing a first draft	4 sessions over a week
☐ Reviewing and revising your draft	2 sessions over a week
☐ Finalizing and submitting your essay	1 day
	Total time needed: Approximately 4 weeks

Selecting a topic

After reviewing the requirements of the assignment you should be able to select a topic in a day or so. You may already have a topic in mind or your tutor may have assigned a specific topic in which case you can skip this step. If you find yourself taking longer than a day or two to select a topic you may want to speak to your tutor and get some additional guidance so you don't fall behind schedule.

Locating sources

Depending on the topic, for an essay you should be able to locate enough source information within a couple of days.

For other more comprehensive projects, locating sources will take more time. If you are working on a thesis or dissertation this step could take months. You will need to think about the requirements and the amount of information you need to include in your writing to estimate the time it will take to locate enough source information.

Reviewing sources and taking notes

This example estimates about a week to review sources and take notes. Be mindful that you will also need to take into consideration how fast you read and take notes! Fast readers may do this more quickly. If you like to take more time when you read, or read things multiple times as I sometimes do, you will need to account for the extra time in your estimate.

As with locating resources, this step varies with the comprehensiveness of the writing project and you will spend more time on this task with longer writing projects.

Creating an outline

This example estimates a couple of days to prepare an outline for an essay. Keep in mind this task could take longer if you are required to submit an outline to your tutor before writing your first draft. You will also need to think about whether you might need to make revisions to the outline and include the time for this if so.

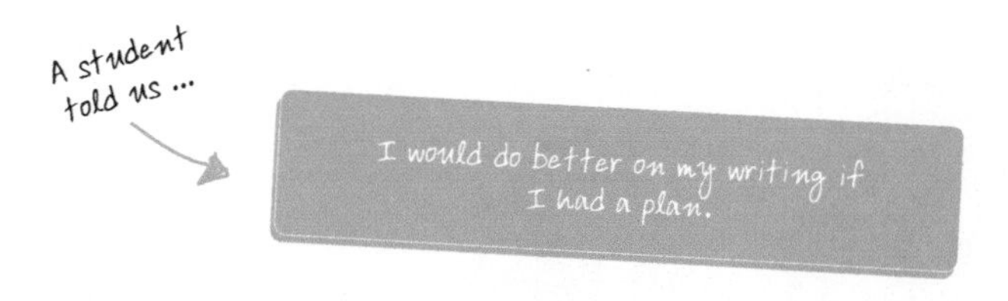

Writing a first draft

This estimate includes 4 sessions over 1 week. How long you spend during each session is up to you. You could break up the sessions by duration or based on the sections of your essay, like this:

- Session 1 – Complete the introduction
- Session 2 – Work on the body
- Session 3 – Complete the body
- Session 4 – Complete the conclusion.

While this example relates to an essay, you can apply the same concepts to longer, more comprehensive writing assignments by extending the time to complete the first draft. You can use a similar approach for mapping out the sessions and aligning them to the major parts of your assignment.

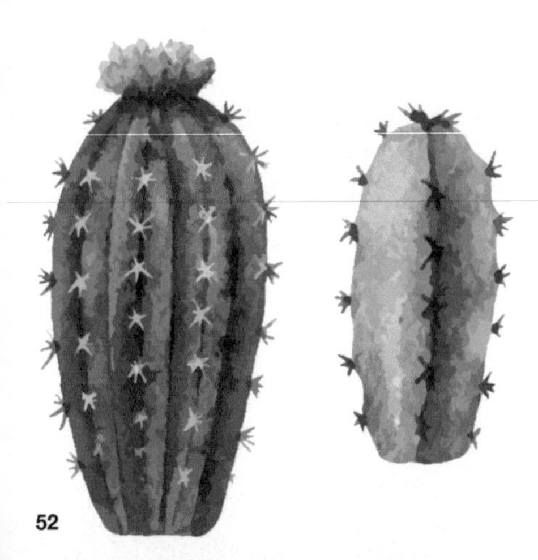

Reviewing and revising your draft

Now that your first draft is complete you will probably only need a few sessions to review the draft for cohesiveness and to address any spelling mistakes and grammar issues.

Do plan for more time if you will need to submit your first draft and receive feedback from your tutor or from a peer reviewer.

Finalizing and submitting your essay

By planning your writing tasks your essay should be in good shape and require minimal time for final review and submission.

Determining the total time

Now that you've estimated the time for each task youhave an idea of how long the entire process will take. This helps you know when to start your assignment in order to submit it on time. You also need to know this for the setting task completion phase of the PSTI process, which we discuss in the next section.

What if I have a big writing project?

While the example in this section discusses how to plan writing tasks for an essay, the same approach can be used for longer writing assignments:

- Determine the major parts of your project as well as reviewing the writing process
- List all of the tasks as in the essay example
- Estimate the timing for each task.

Congratulations

on planning your writing tasks!

Put the steps for planning tasks in order by writing numbers 1–4 in front of each task. Place number 1 in front of the task that should be done first, number 2 in front of the second task. Continue this process to show the correct order for the tasks below.

____Estimate how much time it will take to do each task

____Make a list of all upcoming writing assignments

____Look ahead to see what writing assignments are due

____Detail the tasks you will need to do for each writing assignment

Answers:

_4__Estimate how much time it will take to do each task

_2__Make a list of all upcoming writing assignments

_1__Look ahead to see what writing assignments are due

_3__Detail the tasks you will need to do for each writing assignment

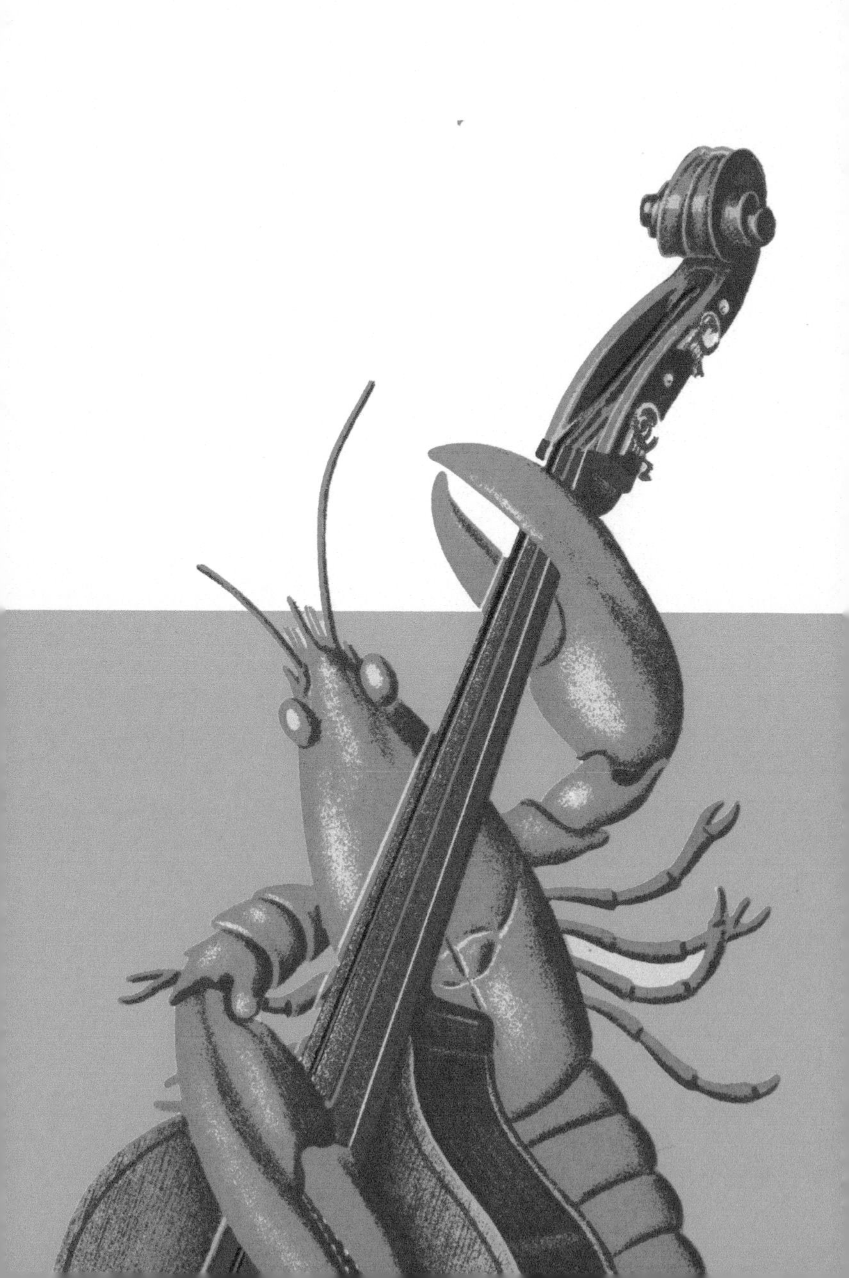

SECTION SIX

How do I set task completion deadlines?

10 second summary

You will use the task completion estimates to set your deadlines.

60 second summary

Know how long tasks will take

Now that you have estimated how long it will take to compete each task, we will use this information to set task completion deadlines. In this step you will set a task completion deadline based on how long it will take to complete a task.

Having reviewed task completion estimates, you will look at a calendar and select dates by which to complete tasks. It may be helpful to write down those dates. Review the list and make sure timelines are feasible and realistic for your schedule. Be sure to confirm that the dates you select will allow you enough time complete and submit assignments on time. You can also follow this process to assign tasks and completion deadlines if you are working with a partner or in a group.

What exactly will I do in the first part of the setting task completion deadlines?

In the first part of the setting task completion deadlines phase of P**S**TI you will:

- Ensure timelines are realistic
- Assign task completion deadlines.

We will continue our essay example and use the existing task estimates to set task completion deadlines. In this step, you will:

- Review the task estimates
- Review a calendar
- Select days to work on and complete tasks
- Write down the dates by which you will complete each task, based on the task completion estimate
- If working in a group or with a partner, assign tasks accordingly.

Tackle your writing project one step at a time!

What about tasks that takes multiple days to complete?

When you work on a task that will take multiple days to complete, the last day you write down is the deadline or the day by which the task needs to be completed. Be sure to review the timelines to ensure they are feasible and allow you to submit your writing assignment on time. Let's say our essay is due on 9 October – the example below allows us to submit the essay on that date.

- Realistic timeline: Start work on an essay 3–4 weeks before it is due.
- Unrealistic timeline: Start work on an essay 1 week before it is due.
- Very unrealistic timeline: Start work on an essay the day before it is due.

An example of writing in the dates is as follows:

Essay writing tasks	**Time estimate**	**Date**
☐ Selecting a topic	1 day	14/9
☐ Locating sources (e.g. articles, books, appropriate websites)	2 days	16-17/9
☐ Reviewing sources and taking notes	4 sessions over a week	21/9, 23/9, 24/9, 25/9
☐ Creating an outline	2 days	28-29/9
☐ Writing a first draft	4 sessions over a week	30/9, 1/10, 2/10, 4/10
☐ Reviewing and revising your draft	2 sessions over a week	6-7/10
☐ Finalizing and submitting your essay	1 day	9/10

A student told us ...

I sometimes get overwhelmed when I have a big writing assignment.

Estimating skills

The time it takes to complete a writing assignment varies depending on the type of project. Review the time estimates in the box below and fill in the time estimates for completing each project.

Time estimates		
4 weeks	1 year	2 hours

__________ An essay

__________ A discussion board post

__________ A thesis or dissertation

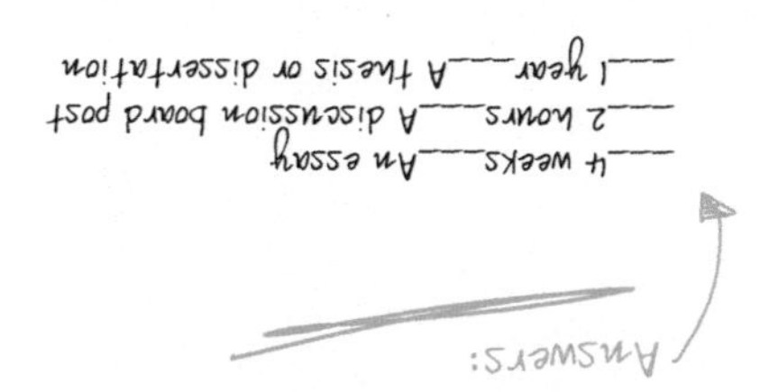

SECTION SEVEN

How do I stay on track and make sure everything gets done?

10 second summary

You will add writing tasks to a calendar to help you see what is coming up and keep you on track, making sure everything gets done.

10

60 second summary

Use a calendar to stay on track

Now that you have assigned dates and deadlines for writing tasks we will add these items to a calendar and set reminders. Using the calendar and reminder feature on your smartphone or computer will help you keep track of upcoming tasks.

In the second part of the setting task completion phase of P**S**TI, you will do the following:

- Review list of tasks with completion dates
- Add dates to the calendar on your phone or computer
- Decide when you want to be reminded of upcoming tasks and set reminders.

What is an example of adding tasks to a calendar?

We will continue with our essay example and use the list of tasks with completion dates. In this step you will:

- Determine which calendar app you will use
- Review the features of the app and make sure you know how to create events in the app
- Create a new event for each task and add it to the calendar based on the date
- Determine when you want to be reminded of the upcoming event and set a reminder/alert.

When should I be reminded?

Setting reminders is a personal preference. As a suggestion, set the reminder based on how long it will take you to do the task.

For example, if you can complete a task in a few hours on 1 day, set the reminder for the day before. If you will work on a task over multiple days in a week, such as 4 sessions in 1 week to complete a rough draft of an essay, set the reminder for a week prior. This will remind you that you will be spending a lot of your time during the upcoming week working on the rough draft.

Plan now so you don't forget later!

An example of the essay writing tasks in a calendar is as follows:

September 2020

< Today >

Sun	Mon	Tue	Wed	Thu	Fri	Sat
30	31	Sep 1	2	3	4	5
6	7 Labor Day	8	9	10	11	12
13	14 • Select topic 9 AM	15	16 • Locate sources 11 AM	17 • Locate sources 11 AM	18	19 Rosh Hashanah
20	21 • Review/take notes 9 AM	22	23 • Review/take not... 9 AM	24 • Review/take not... 9 AM	25 • Review/take not... 9 AM	26
27 Yom Kippur	28 • Outline 9 AM	29 • Outline 9 AM	30 • First draft 9 AM	Oct 1 • First draft 9 AM	2 • First draft 9 AM	3
4 • First draft 9 AM	5	6 • Revise 9 AM	7 • Revise 9 AM	8	9 • Submit essay 9 AM	10

This example was taken from an iOS Mac computer

7:46

Sep 2020

S	M	T	W	T	F	S
		1	2	3	4	5
6	7	8	9	10	11	12
13	14	15	16	17	18	19
20	21	22	23	24	25	26
27	28	29	30			

9:00 AM
10:00 AM
Select topic

4:00 PM
5:00 PM
Group 5 meeting (all members)

This example was taken from an iOS iPhone.

In summary, adding writing tasks to a calendar and setting reminders helps you track upcoming tasks and helps you make sure you get everything done.

For adding tasks to a calendar and setting reminders

- [ ] Create a new event for each task.
- [ ] Set a reminder/alert.
- [ ] Add tasks to your calendar.

A student told us …

I sometimes forget what I need to do.

Making use of calendars

Work through the following questions to plan using calendars:

1. Which calendar app will you use?

2. How far in advance do you need to be reminded of upcoming tasks?

SECTION EIGHT

How do I take action to complete tasks?

10 second summary

You will incorporate strategies to maintain accountability to yourself and establish a sense of integrity to ensure you take action to follow through and complete tasks.

60 second summary

Ways to establish accountability and integrity to complete writing tasks

Now that you have set task completion deadlines, added these items to a calendar and set reminders, we will discuss strategies to make sure you follow through and complete writing tasks.

In the taking action phase of PS**T**I you will use strategies including minimizing multitasking, setting goals and establishing an accountability contract with yourself. Key to this is having a sense of integrity in the process. Integrity is simply committing to do what you said you would do. Avoiding multitasking helps you focus on effectively completing one task at a time. Setting weekly and daily goals helps to ensure you continue to work on completing tasks each day. Entering into an accountability contract builds integrity into the process as a promise you make to yourself that you will follow through.

Implementing strategies

Using the following strategies can help you make sure you follow through with completing tasks:

- Focus on completing one task at a time
- Set weekly and daily goals
- Cross tasks off your list as you complete them
- Create an accountability contract with yourself
- Reward yourself when you complete a writing assignment.

Why should I focus on completing one task at a time?

Multitasking in general causes you to split your attention between two tasks and neither task is done effectively. For example, have you ever tried to send a text message while talking on the phone? Sometimes the person you are talking to will ask if you are still there because they can sense you are distracted. The same holds true for your writing tasks. Focus your attention and complete one task at a time.

Why should I set goals?

Setting weekly and daily goals is another strategy for following through with completing tasks. At the beginning of each week, review your calendar and write some weekly goals. Then at the beginning of each day, write down some goals for the day that will help you complete your writing tasks.

In your goal statement, simply state *what you will do* and *by when*.

Examples:

Weekly goal: This week I will complete my rough draft.

By when   What you will do

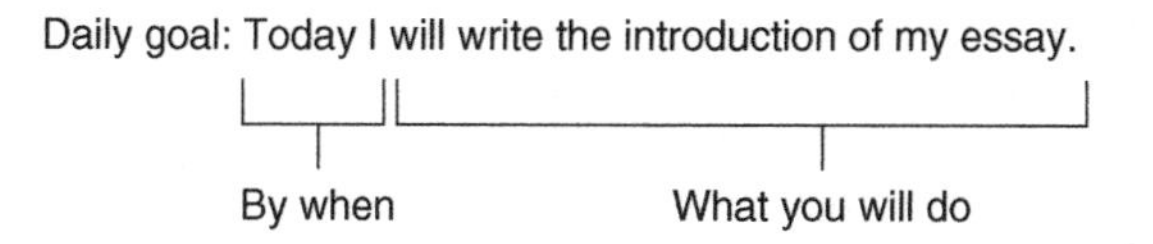

Why is it helpful to cross off completed tasks?

Crossing off completed tasks helps you track what has been completed and shows what still needs to be done. Additionally, it feels good to cross things off your list! It gives you a sense of accomplishment. It is like a small win that adds up to the big win of completing your writing assignment. Achieving the daily and weekly goals shows that you are making progress towards the ultimate goal of completing the assignment, so you can see a light at the end of the tunnel. You can use written checklists or Excel to keep track of this.

Essay writing tasks	**Time estimate**	**Date**
☐ ~~Selecting a topic~~	~~1 day~~	~~14/9~~
☐ ~~Locating sources (e.g. articles, books, appropriate websites)~~	~~2 days~~	~~16–17/9~~
☐ ~~Reviewing sources and taking notes~~	~~4 sessions over a week~~	~~21/9, 23/9, 24/9, 25/9~~
☐ Creating an outline	2 days	28–29/9
☐ Writing a first draft	4 sessions over a week	30/9, 1/10, 2/10, 4/10
☐ Reviewing and revising your draft	2 sessions over a week	6–7/10
☐ Finalizing and submitting your essay	1 day	9/10

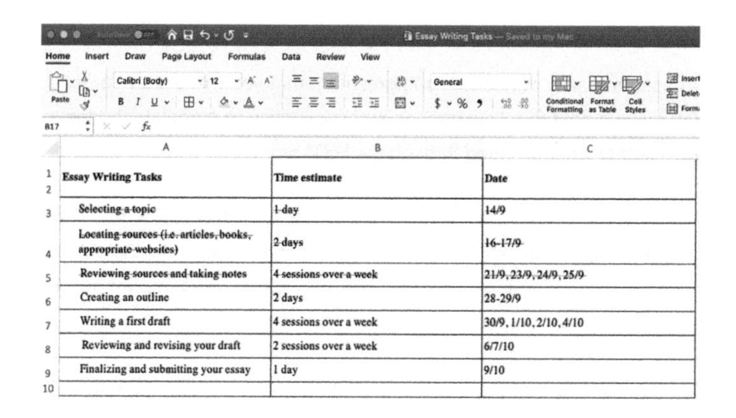

Essay Writing Tasks	Time estimate	Date
~~Selecting a topic~~	~~1 day~~	~~14/9~~
~~Locating sources (i.e. articles, books, appropriate websites)~~	~~2 days~~	~~16-17/9~~
~~Reviewing sources and taking notes~~	~~4 sessions over a week~~	~~21/9, 23/9, 24/9, 25/9~~
Creating an outline	2 days	28-29/9
Writing a first draft	4 sessions over a week	30/9, 1/10, 2/10, 4/10
Reviewing and revising your draft	2 sessions over a week	6/7/10
Finalizing and submitting your essay	1 day	9/10

Used with permission from Microsoft.

Each small win adds up to a big win!

How can I create an accountability contract?

An accountability contract is an agreement that you make with yourself. You make a pact to follow through and take action to complete the tasks you identify when working through the PSTI process.

Accountability contracts do not need to be long and elaborate. They are just simple statements that detail your commitment to taking action. Accountability contracts are a reminder that you entered into an agreement and you should follow through on your word.

It is recommended that you complete a new contract at the start of each semester or term to refresh the commitment to follow through.

Example:

I ______________________________ agree to use the PSTI process to manage my time during my writing projects. I agree to plan tasks, set task completion deadlines, take action to complete tasks and honour my integrity to follow through all phases of the process. I agree to review upcoming tasks, complete tasks and submit my assignments on time.

______________________________(Signature) ______________(Date)

Why should I reward myself?

You should reward yourself with something you enjoy when you complete a writing project. It is not meant to be elaborate or expensive but just a little treat for yourself. Your reward could be a trip to the cinema, a quick trip to the beach if you are near one, or a picnic in the park.

Determine what your reward will be when you start your writing project and enjoy the reward when you complete the project. This will give you something additional to enjoy and work towards earning.

Integrity makes everything work

Integrity in the PSTI process is like updating the operating system on your computer or phone. It ensures the PSTI process works properly and keeps the process moving. This means completing every phase of the PSTI process to manage your time.

Following the PSTI process helps ensure you have enough time to properly plan and complete your writing assignments. Devoting time to ensure you meet all the requirements of an assignment can improve the quality of your work.

How can I make sure I successfully manage my time with writing projects?

- When starting a new writing project, review the phases of PSTI.
- Review your accountability contract.
- Follow the PSTI process.
- Check your calendar for upcoming tasks.
- Write weekly and daily goals.
- Reward yourself for completing writing assignments on time.

Accountability contract template

Use this template to create your accountability contract at the start of each semester/term. Feel free to modify it if there are more items you would like to add.

> I ___________________________ agree to use the PSTI process to manage my time during my writing projects. I agree to plan tasks, set task completion deadlines, take action to complete tasks, and honour my integrity to follow through all phases of the process. I agree to review upcoming tasks, complete tasks and submit my assignments on time.
>
> ___________________________(Signature) _________________(Date)

Congratulations

on learning and detailing strategies to make sure you take action to complete your writing tasks!

SECTION NINE

How do I manage my time when working with a partner or in a group?

10 second summary

When working in a group or with a partner, you will follow the PSTI process in the same way as when working on individual projects. You will include an additional step to assign tasks and incorporate a group or partner accountability contract.

60 second summary

PSTI for groups

Some students dread working in groups because they are concerned about other group members not doing their share of the work. The PSTI process is very helpful when working in a group as it helps to make sure all members are aware of what needs to be done. Follow the PSTI process in the same way as when you work on solo projects.

You will need to incorporate project meetings as well as include some additional steps in phases of the PSTI process. Some of the additional steps unique to working in groups include assigning tasks to group members. Like the individual accountability contract, creating an accountability contract with group members will help to ensure that everyone follows through with completing their assigned tasks.

Working in groups

When working in groups or with a partner you will need to add some additional steps which include:

- Incorporating project meetings
- Adding some additional steps to some phases of the PSTI process.

During the first meeting explain the PSTI process to your partner or other group members. As a suggestion, you can use the outline below to guide your first meeting. Time management is a valuable tool for everyone so you may want to suggest that group members purchase their own copy of this book and work through the activities to learn the process fully.

I don't like working in groups because I end up doing all the work.

Suggested outline for first meeting

- Planning tasks
  - Look ahead to see what writing assignments are due
  - Make a list of all upcoming writing assignments
  - Assign tasks to group members
  - Determine how much time writing tasks will take.
- Setting task completion deadlines
  - Ensure timelines are realistic
  - Schedule writing tasks on a calendar
    - Include reminders and who is responsible for completing tasks.
- Taking action to complete tasks
  - Follow through with completing tasks
  - Set weekly goals for the group
  - Cross tasks off your list as group members complete tasks
  - Create an accountability contract with group members
  - Track the status of task completion.
- Integrity
  - Have personal responsibility and be accountable – do what you said you would do during every step of PSTI.

Include weekly check-ins with group members or your partner to review upcoming items, and discuss what has been completed and the overall status of the project.

What additional steps do I need to do during the planning tasks phase?

During the planning tasks phase you will need to assign tasks to your partner or group members. Simply add a column to the task planning table and include the name of the group member who is responsible for completing the task. It's a good idea to have a list of tasks for your group and your own list as well.

Example of adding tasks for group members working on a writing project:

Essay writing tasks	Responsible group member	Time estimate	Date
☐ Group meeting #1 (overview of PSTI, assign sections)	All group members	1 day	14/9
☐ Write report	Sam Steve	1 week	21/9
☐ Create presentation	Nicole	1 week	28/9

What additional steps do I need to do during the setting task completion deadlines phase?

Create or share a calendar with your partner or group members. Include who is responsible for completing tasks when adding tasks to a calendar, like this:

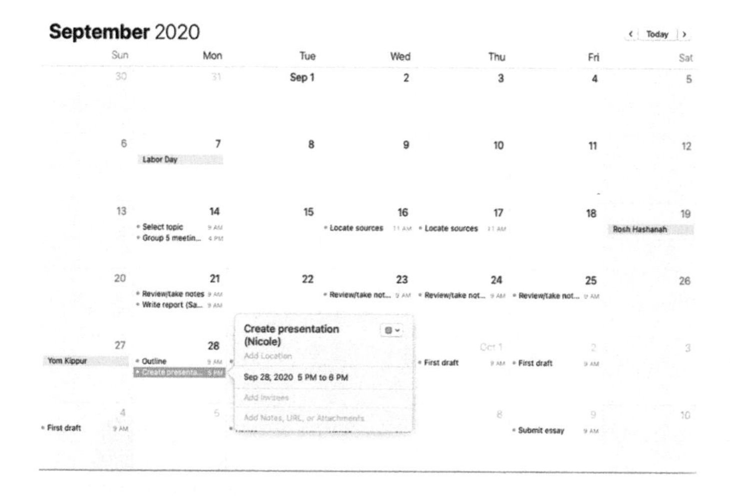

This example was taken from an iOS Mac computer.

What additional steps do I need to take during the taking action to complete tasks phase?

Incorporating a group accountability contract is helpful to make sure everyone agrees to complete their assigned tasks. Using a group accountability contract reminds group members of their expectations to complete the group assignment. It is a useful tool for ensuring group work is equitable.

Accountability contract template

Use this template to create an accountability contract with your group members. Feel free to modify it if there are more items you would like to add!

The members of this group include:

____________________, ____________________, ____________________

who have been assigned to work on ______________________________.

We as a group agree to use the PSTI process to manage our time during our writing project. We agree to plan tasks, set task completion deadlines, take action to complete tasks and honour our integrity to follow through all phases of the process. We agree to meet weekly to review upcoming tasks, to complete tasks and to submit our assignment on time.

__________________________(Signature) ____________________(Date)

__________________________(Signature) ____________________(Date)

__________________________(Signature) ____________________(Date)

What are some tips for working with group members?

Tips for working with others include:

- Treat others as you wish to be treated
- Set expectations from the beginning of the project by reviewing the requirements of the assignment and following the PSTI process
- Be sure to have weekly meetings and discuss the status of the project and see if anyone is having any difficulties
- Encourage open communication
- Refer back to the group's weekly goals and ensure everyone is on target for meeting goals.

> Group work works best when you work together!

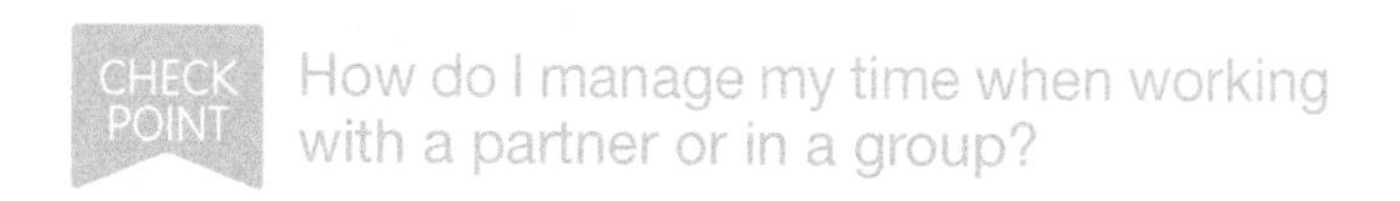

Review each of the statements below and determine if they describe time management strategies for working in groups.

1. During the planning phase, assign tasks to your partner or group members
2. Use a group accountability contract to remind group members of their expectations to complete the group assignment
3. If you have a group accountability contract, it is not necessary to meet with group members
4. Schedule writing tasks and who is responsible for completing them on a calendar

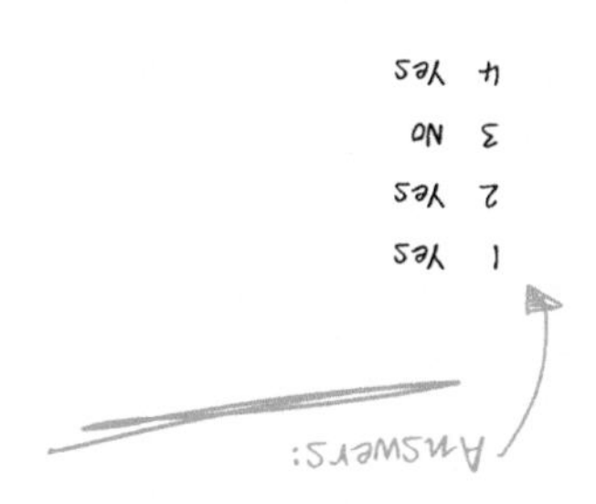

SECTION TEN

How do I manage my time while balancing academic and other life priorities?

10 second summary

You can apply the PSTI process to manage all your time to help balance academic responsibilities and other life priorities.

60 second summary

Balance is the key

As we previously learnt, your life is made up of the following types of tasks:

- Essential – things that you must get done (e.g. eating, paying bills, attending lectures)
- Compelling – things that are important to you and enrich your life (e.g. cultural or faith-based activities, voluntary work, helping a friend)
- Leisure – things you do for fun or to relax (e.g. going to the cinema, going out to eat, listening to music).

It will be essential to balance your schedule in order to get all the essential tasks done but still to find time for other types of tasks.

How do I balance it all?

You may sometimes feel overwhelmed trying to balance everything.

- Writing an essay
- Work
- Attending lectures

- Volunteering
- Going on a date

Applying the PSTI process can help you manage it all. You will follow the PSTI process in the same way as when you work on writing projects. However, you will add some additional steps to two phases of the process:

- Planning tasks
- Setting task completion deadlines

I feel burnout when I focus too much on work and I don't do anything fun.

What additional steps do I need to take?

In addition to the writing tasks, also look ahead and identify other essential, compelling and leisure tasks. Next, follow the steps of the PSTI process and plan these tasks in the same way.

Add these tasks to your calendar as you would for a writing task. You may find it helpful to colour-code tasks: if you have a job you could choose blue to schedule your work hours. This way you can easily see the days that you work.

You can pick other colours to represent assignments due in different modules. There are many ways to colour-code tasks, so think about a system that works best for you.

In this example:

- Blue = work responsibilities
- Light green = essay writing
- Orange = group work
- Dark green = social activities

September 2020

‹ Today ›

Sun	Mon	Tue	Wed	Thu	Fri	Sat
30	31	Sep 1	2	3	4	5
6	7 Labor Day	8 • Work: Evening S... 5 PM	9	10	11	12
13	14 • Select topic 9 AM • Group 5 meetin... 4 PM	15 • Work: Evening S... 5 PM	16 • Locate sources 11 AM	17 • Locate sources 11 AM • Help Friend move 5 PM	18 • Work: Evening S... 9 AM	19 Rosh Hashanah
20	21 • Review/take notes 9 AM • Write report (Sa... 9 AM	22 • Work: Evening S... 5 PM	23 • Review/take not... 9 AM	24 • Review/take not... 9 AM	25 • Review/take not... 9 AM • Work: Evening S... 9 AM	26
27 Yom Kippur	28 • Outline 9 AM • Create presenta... 5 PM	29 • Outline 9 AM • Work: Evening S... 5 PM	30 • First draft 9 AM	Oct 1 • First draft 9 AM	2 • First draft 9 AM • Work: Evening S... 9 AM	3
4 • First draft 9 AM	5	6 • Revise 9 AM • Work: Evening S... 5 PM	7 • Revise 9 AM	8	9 • Submit essay 9 AM • Work: Evening S... 9 AM	10

How do I prioritize tasks?

When you're planning and scheduling tasks you may find that you don't have time to do everything that you planned in a given week. If this happens you will need to prioritize by deciding which tasks are the most important to complete.

Prioritize tasks by categorizing each as essential, compelling or leisure. First find time for the essential tasks, then find space for compelling and leisure tasks. Keep in mind that you may have to decide between completing certain tasks. Do be mindful that a bit of leisure is needed so as far as possible don't eliminate leisure tasks completely. On the flip side, don't spend all of your time doing leisure tasks and neglect attending to essential tasks!

It's all about planning the right balance!

CHECK POINT How do I balance it all?

Let's check your understanding of it all. Test your knowledge by answering the following questions.

1. How do I manage my time while balancing academic and other life priorities?
2. What additional steps do I need to take during the planning tasks phase?
3. What additional steps do I need to take during the setting task completion deadlines phase?
4. How do I prioritize tasks?

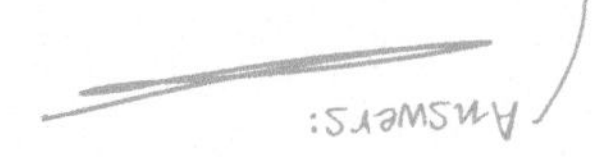

1. Follow the PSTI process and add steps for planning tasks and setting task completion deadlines.
2. In addition to the writing tasks, look ahead and identify other essential, compelling and leisure tasks. Next, follow the steps of the PSTI process and plan these tasks in the same way.
3. Add these tasks to your calendar as you would for a writing task. You may find it helpful to colour-code tasks.
4. Prioritize tasks by thinking about what is essential, compelling and leisure. Prioritize the essential tasks, then find space for compelling and leisure tasks.

Congratulations

on learning skills to manage time in all areas of your life!

SECTION ELEVEN

DIY: Putting it all together

Work through the following activities to think more deeply about how you spend your time and construct a plan of action for the future.

1 What are the tasks in your life?

Take some time and reflect on all the tasks that make up your life and add them to the category where you feel they belong.

Note: There is no right or wrong answer. A task that you may find essential may be compelling for someone else.

Essential	Compelling	Leisure

2 Assessing your writing assignments

Take a moment to review your modules and the course as a whole.

1. Highlight all the writing assignments.
2. Think about what level of learning each writing assignment evaluates.
3. Write down the writing assignment in the column that corresponds to the level of learning it assesses.

Concept or topic level	Module level	Course level

3 What are some of the ways you've mismanaged your time when writing in the past?

Think back to some of your past writing projects. Were there any times where you procrastinated or didn't prepare properly? Ask yourself ...

1 What were the types of writing projects?

2 How did you procrastinate?

3 For your next assignment, list three steps you will take to ensure you manage your time better:

4 How can you use PSTI to manage your time for writing projects?

Thinking about your next writing project, how can you use the PSTI process to manage your time better? List three things you will do for each step of the process.

Planning tasks

1 ______________________________

2 ______________________________

3 ______________________________

Setting task completion deadlines

1 ______________________________

2 ______________________________

3 ______________________________

Taking action to complete tasks

1 ______________________________

2 ______________________________

3 ______________________________

Integrity

1 ______________________________

2 ______________________________

3 ______________________________

5 What do I need to do in my next writing assignment?

1. Review your modules and select an upcoming writing assignment.
2. Using the space below, consider these questions:
   a. What is the writing assignment?

   ____

   ____

   b. Do I need to do research?

   ____

   ____

   c. What type of writing process will I use to structure and write my paper?

   ____

   ____

   d. What do I need to do before I can start writing?

   ____

   ____

3. Estimate the time it will take to complete each stage of the writing task. Using the table below, add up the total time to estimate how long it will take to complete the entire writing assignment.

Writing tasks	Estimated time	Date
☐		
☐		
☐		
☐		
☐		
☐		
☐		
☐		
☐		
☐		
☐		
☐		
☐	**Total time needed:**	

6 How will you establish and maintain accountability?

Review the ways of establishing and maintaining accountability to complete writing tasks. Using the space below, detail 3 strategies you will implement and how.

Strategy 1:

How will you implement this?

Strategy 2:

How will you implement this?

Strategy 3:

How will you implement this?

Final checklist: How to know you are done

Planning tasks

- Have you looked ahead and made a list of everything that needs to be done? ☐
- Have you determined how much time each task will take and prioritized tasks as needed? ☐

Setting task completion deadlines

- Have you set realistic timeframes and scheduled tasks in a calendar? ☐

Taking action to complete tasks

- Have you set daily and weekly goals for completing tasks? ☐
- Have you created and followed an accountability contract? ☐
- Are you tracking the status of your completion by crossing tasks off your list once completed? ☐

Integrity

- Are you being accountable during every step of PSTI? ☐

Glossary

Accountability Taking personal responsibility to complete tasks.

Accountability contract An agreement that you make with yourself and/or others that you will follow through and take action to complete the tasks you identify when working through the PSTI process.

Compelling tasks Things that are important to you and enrich your life (e.g. cultural or faith-based activities, voluntary work, helping a friend).

Essential tasks Tasks that you must complete (e.g. eating, paying bills, attending lectures).

Integrity Part of the PSTI process that means being accountable and doing what you said you would do during every step.

Leisure tasks Activities done for fun or to relax (e.g. going to the cinema, going out to eat, listening to music).

Long-term memory A function of the brain responsible for storing information for a long time. Here, information is remembered and not easily forgotten. Learning happens when information moves into the long-term memory.

Management To use strategies to make sure something operates properly and runs smoothly.

Planning tasks A step in the PSTI process that involves identifying what needs to be done and detailing those tasks.

PSTI process A quick and easy time management process where each letter stands for a step in the overall process:

- Planning tasks
- Setting task completion deadlines
- Taking action to complete tasks
- Integrity.

Setting task completion deadlines A step in the PSTI process that involves determining realistic timelines and scheduling tasks.

Short-term memory A function of the brain to store information for a short time. If information is not further processed, it will be forgotten.

Taking action A step in the PSTI process that involves following through to complete tasks and tracking the status of task completion.

Time management Using strategies to manage your time by thoughtfully identifying and planning when you will complete tasks.

Writing process A high-level process for completing the major sections of various types of academic writing assignments.

Further resources

There are many resources to help you with the overall writing process, whether you are writing an essay, literature review or a thesis or dissertation. You may want to read other titles in the Super Quick Skills series such as:

- *Plan Your Essay* by Phillip C. Shon
- *Find Your Source* by Gary Thomas
- *Cite Your Source* by Phillip C. Shon
- *Polish Your Academic Writing* by Helen Coleman

Time management tips for busy university students at www.purdueglobal.edu/blog/student-life/time-management-busy-college-students provides some additional strategies for helping students balance academic and life priorities.